Gift to:_____

From:_____

XOXO

BECAUSE
OF
YOU

Eliana

authorHOUSE'

AuthorHouse™
1663 Liberty Drive
Bloomington, IN 47403
www.authorhouse.com
Phone: 833-262-8899

Published by AuthorHouse 11/08/2024

ISBN: 979-8-8230-3591-0 (sc)
ISBN: 979-8-8230-3592-7 (e)

Library of Congress Control Number: 2024923663

Print information available on the last page.

Any people depicted in stock imagery provided by Getty Images are models, and such images are being used for illustrative purposes only. Certain stock imagery © Getty Images.

This book is printed on acid-free paper.

Because of the dynamic nature of the Internet, any web addresses or links contained in this book may have changed since publication and may no longer be valid. The views expressed in this work are solely those of the author and do not necessarily reflect the views of the publisher, and the publisher hereby disclaims any responsibility for them.

ACKNOWLEDGMENTS

I want to express my deepest gratitude to Misha for being my muse! Your presence brought light to my life and let me discover myself! Your unwavering support and encouragement have been the guiding power behind all my new creations. Your belief in me and inspiring presence have fueled my creativity and passion for words. This book is a testament to your influence on my journey. Thank you for being part of my life and allowing me to be part of yours! My endless love goes to eternity.

I extend my sincerest appreciation to Katarina Naskovski, whose unique work and patience in putting together the designs have added a vibrant and dynamic dimension to this book, surpassing my wildest imagination. My gratitude extends to the work and all the days your support and belief in me made the process possible!

I am profoundly grateful to the dedicated team at AuhtorsHouse, starting from Annabelle Mendez and Eve Ardell, for their exceptional expertise, guidance, and unwavering commitment to bringing this poetry book to fruition.

I want to express my heartfelt thanks to my pillars, Dina, Andreea, Kristina, and Brety for letting me be part of your journey.
The following pages will include the days we laughed together, the tears, and the experiences we shared through the years! I love you all; you are a part of my soul!

My gratitude goes to Ashima Ahmed for giving me the time and space from the busy days to find peace and create! You are the backbone I have always needed. Bless you in the years to come.

I am forever grateful to my parents; you are my beginning and end! Mom, for all the nights and mornings you insisted on starting with the books; the world beyond ours was another life to discover; Dad, for always believing in all my creations and giving me support from the beginning!

So, here it is, all *BECAUSE OF YOU*

Bless you all,

Eliana

TABLE OF CONTENTS

BECAUSE OF YOU

The smile that makes my
Fingers run trough your hair,
The heartbeat, which lets
My lips, lock in yours
The soul, which sends
My sight in our world
And beyond…

Because of you, I see
The sunrise is brighter,
Because of you,
I find peace in a rough sea,
Because of you,
My heartbeat is happy,
Because of you,
I find truly me.

A NEW BEGINNING

Time goes up and down,
It has no plan to stop,
The world turned upside down,
All gloomy and grey.

Silent & still,
Life passes by,
Can we do something about,
We can hardly try...

Then, you came around,
Made all colors bright,
Let my heart laugh,
All day & all night.

Blessed you shall be,
For bringing back the sunshine,
Turning all the light up,
In this life of mine.

BECAUSE OF YOU

DANCE WITH TIME

A dream I have
Of magic power
To ask the time
To stop

A kind request to
Biggest rival,
The best of friends
To bind its ticking hands

Once time is gone
Today I have
To kiss the lips
I love

No clock to bind us,
No chasing minutes,
We savor every touch

In world time free
We have forever
And dreams
Are just reality

DO YOU KNOW MY NAME

Do you know my name,
Or only my heart?
Do you know my days,
The hours apart?

Silence broken,
By blending lips,
Words hardly spoken,
Fingers searching,
Looks fast forgotten...

Do you know my name,
Or only my eyes,
Searching for you,
In the lonely nights

Foggy mornings,
Brighter rays,
Is it real,
or goes away by the day?

I WANNA BE

I wanna be the summer,
Toss the sun in
My hair made of clouds,
I wanna be the summer days,
Spreading rays and giggles
Washing the waves
On the burning sand.
I wanna be the sunshine
Joyful knowing
Where the clouds go
Riding the sky.
I wanna be the summer rain
Powerful and fresh
Life-giving and passionate
Wet kisses under
The summer sky.
I wanna be..

LIQUID LOVE

A Soul from the sun
The Sun from the Soul
Its liquid love
That makes us all
The birds in the sky,
The clouds above,
The mountains below,
The hearts inside us,
We all come together
from liquid love,
the one lives forever.
The one that makes us all.

BECAUSE OF YOU

IN YOUR EYES

In your soul, I find my
corner, in quiet peace
and so much joy
The world in there,
Is blast of colors,
A child's laughter
An endless sea

Your eyes in silence
Can whisper secrets,
They tell me stories
I want to know

The words unspoken,
The time unfinished
And every look,
I want it all!

HURRY TIME

I miss you in the evening lights
Day stretched in weeks again,
I miss you in the morning sun,
In search for you...
Where have you gone?
I miss your eyes,
The world between your arms
The softest voice,
The beat of your heart
I miss to find
My world in yours,
So, hurry time!!!

IN YOUR ARMS

In your arms
There is a blissful world
In stormy days.
In your arms
The Sun sets in joy
Searching for the morning after
In your arms
I wanna dance
In silence so loud,
Kiss time, break rules,
Bend life to discover
My world.

PIECE OF ME

DEDICATED TO MY BEST DINA

The days are passing so fast
Not sure where the time flies,
Life becomes a thing from the past
And the Sun remains to shine

Looking back I see,
Those days are blessed continually,
Having the best could possibly be,
A friend then, now, and to be!

Standing front, right, and back,
In a storm, broken heart, or pure luck,
I pray all the humankind,
Get to see a friendship like yours and mine!

PLEASE HANDLE WITH CARE

Promise to handle with care,
And keep us together,
Summer nights,
Into the dark blue sky

Sticky lips,
Blended hearts, souls twisted,
Yet days mostly
Apart

Please handle with care,
Like the sky manages stars,
Bright, but breakable,
Yet full of light in the night.

Never let go kisses,
Fingertips crossed forever,
Hearts over each other,
Eyes speak louder than words.

Please handle with care,
A bubble or diamond glass...

THAT THING CALLED...LIFE

DEDICATED TO ANDREEA

Sitting in a quiet room,
Wondering where the time goes,
The sun is set, the day is gone,
And "what if" is in your thought

"What if" is never real,
"What if" is just a game
"What if" is in position,
To let you take the blame!

Remember fearless,
You ARE, you conquered
heavy days,
Remember life has shown you,
Love in many ways

"What if" is a deception
A non-existent foe,
No power is required,
From you to let it go!!!

The days are somehow quiet,
The sun is shining bright,
You don't need me to
Remind you how loved you are!

THE ECLIPSE

The sky is blue, the sun is bright.
Wondering how to
Blend with the night.

The sun needs the moon,
The moon needs the light,
It's really lonely,
Despite stary night.

Thunder and storm,
Brakes in the sky,
Getting together
The forces of life.

This is where time STOPS!!!
And the world stands by
Watching in awe
Their kiss in the sky.

Eclipse in the sky,
Eclipse in the soul,
It's all about life,
Worth living for.

THE FIGHT

Another day, another hour,
The creepy darkness
Comes to me.
A ray of light,
Your magic power
Arrives on time
To let me be.
Nine hundred years,
Same days revealed,
It seems a fight
As old as life.
How could you've known
That it appears,
How did you find it now?
In Rumi's words
I have discovered,
The fight is always
There to be.
It's our love for life
The power to set
The world forever free

THE NAKED SOUL

Nine thousand days
In joy through darkness,
Nine thousand nights
In search of me

The day arrived,
When I discovered,
It was a blessing
Not a curse

The time elapsed,
The heavy covers,
It was the safest road
To you

The light, the love,
And all the suns,
Released the shield
I built so sharp

And here you have
My heart, my soul
The breath I hold,
The world I know.

And if today
Is last for me,
I know it is for eternity.

BECAUSE OF YOU

THE RED STRING

DEDICATED TO ASHIMA

Sometimes you win,
Sometimes you lose,
In search of string red,
You, child of mine
In voyage unknown,
You think is divine

The love in this life,
Is more than a string
It starts with the sun,
When morning begins,
The peace in our hearts,
The beauty around,
It strengthens in
Rough sea,
In days we believe,
There is more in the world,
We are here to give.

THE STORM

The darkest clouds danced
In passion,
Created storm unseen.
The sea had freedom
To kiss the sky,
And flirted with
The rain.
The trees enjoyed
The love around them,
But twisted in despair.
in days like these,
I sit and wonder,
It's all the same with us.
The love we seek
In storms unknown
In a blend of joy and pain.

THE TRUTH

Like a cat, the sun stretches
over the sky, fluffy clouds,
Innocent silence.
Clueless of its power,
With a heart so big
And so desired...
Time fooled,
It runs the life,
Blinded by its ego,
Forgets the power of the sun
selfishly spreads
Its arms around.
In days as that
We fall in fear,
Unnoticing the truth,
It's not the time,
The place, that's real...
It is all about the dance
Of light, and love
We do conceal...

UNFINISHED

Two scars of failed dreams
Two scars of broken heart,
They kept the life in days,
When breathing was a task.

Two friends became the world,
With all the tasks inside...
The time, the lonely nights,
The stars in moments
Not so bright!

The time with magic hands
created rescue work,
the books, the music
when, the silence
overtook the days.

Then the world started
To change in colors,
 and vibrant light
And the way to contain it
is to spill it outside.

WHY ME?

A silent room, a quiet day
Your text took my thoughts away...
Why loved you are, a question.
You dropped, so here, my love
The answers won't stop:

The mind in your eyes,
The love in your arms,
The beauty of soul,
The fire at heart

You make the days bright,
And making me laugh,
The peace of your voice,
The strength of your heart.

And when we blend,
The world becomes one,
Your power extends,
And makes me alive

THE WORDS

Expressions of heart,
Expressions of mind,
Words can be strong &
can be kind

Promises thrown
Back & forth in time
It might be just words ...
they don't even rhyme

The words can kill,
Or bring us high,
They make a soul rise
Or worlds collide

A mother to child,
A friend to a friend
It's those words in action
They differ in the end

WHEN I AM GONE

When I am gone
In search for me,
You will see me
In a flower petal
My kisses come
With summer sun,
And touches by
The rain
My eyes you will meet
In baby smile,
In purring of a kitten,
My heartbeat goes
In search of love...
The world you grasp
For love, it is I stand
Forever
The days we had,
The days I lived,
It is all I ever be...

Printed in the United States
by Baker & Taylor Publisher Services